5 MINUTE
Sunday School Activities

For Preschoolers

Bible Adventures

Rainbow Publishers

Rainbow Publishers • P.O. Box 261129 • San Diego, CA 92196
www.rainbowpublishers.com

5 MINUTE
Sunday School Activities

For Preschoolers

Bible Adventures

Mary J. Davis

To Larry, as always.
To our children and their families.

5 MINUTE SUNDAY SCHOOL ACTIVITIES FOR PRESCHOOLERS: BIBLE ADVENTURES
©2005 by Rainbow Publishers
ISBN 1-58411-046-5
Rainbow reorder# RB38411
church and ministry/ministry resources/children's ministry

Rainbow Publishers
P.O. Box 261129
San Diego, CA 92196
www.rainbowpublishers.com

Interior Illustrator: Chuck Galey
Cover Illustrator: Todd Marsh

Printed in the United States of America

Contents

Introduction

Children need to grow up learning the foundational lessons of the Bible. Even young preschoolers can begin to learn the basics of God's love and care.

5-Minute Sunday School Activities for Preschoolers is designed to give teachers a quick activity that teaches an important Bible truth. Teachers are often faced with a few extra minutes after the lesson is finished. There are also times when a teacher needs a few moments to get attendance and other important matters out of the way before the main lesson. Instead of wasting these minutes with non-learning play, provide a 5-minute activity for the children.

The activities in the book can also be used as entire lessons. Scriptures, teaching suggestions and memory verses are included with each activity.

As a teacher of young children, you can make these activities go quickly by doing much of the preparatory work before class. You may also make the activities take longer, by allowing children to do their own cutting.

EXTRA TIME suggestions will be given for the activities. If you have more than 5 minutes for children to complete the craft, you may want to choose the extra time suggestion.

God Made Everything
Genesis 1:1-2:3

God created the heavens and the earth.
Genesis 1:1

WHAT YOU NEED

- page 10, duplicated
- crayons

BEFORE CLASS

Duplicate pattern page for each child. Make a sample to show the children.

WHAT TO DO

1. Introduce the lesson by telling the Creation story found in Genesis chapter 1. Say, **God made the world and everything in it. He made the sun, moon and stars. He separated the land and water. Then God filled the waters with fish and the land with plants and animals. Then God made people to live in His world.**
2. Show the children your sample.
3. Distribute a pattern page to each child.
4. Say the memory verse.
5. Have the children trace the broken lines to discover some of God's creations. Then have the children color the pictures as they wish.
6. After the pictures are finished, have the children name some of the things in the creation picture. Also, have the children name some other things that God created.

EXTRA TIME

Provide real nature items or cut-outs from magazines for the children to glue to their pictures.

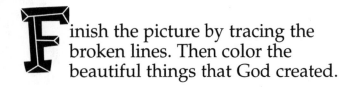 **F**inish the picture by tracing the broken lines. Then color the beautiful things that God created.

God created the heavens and the earth.
Genesis 1:1

God Makes Families
Genesis 2:20-24 and 4:1-2

MEMORY VERSE

The Lord God made a woman...and brought her to the man.
~ Genesis 2:22

WHAT YOU NEED

- page 12, duplicated
- crayons

BEFORE CLASS

Duplicate the pattern page for each child. For younger children, fold the pages on the broken lines. Make a sample to show the children.

WHAT TO DO

1. Introduce the lesson by telling the story found in Genesis 2:20-24 and 4:1-2. Say, **God made a man and called him "Adam." He made a woman who was named Eve. Then Adam and Eve had a son named Cain and another son named Abel. They were the very first family in the world. God makes families.**
2. Show the children the sample.
3. Distribute a pattern page to each child.
4. Say the memory verse.
5. Have the children fold the page on the broken lines and color the pictures on the flaps. Say, **Adam and Eve were the first people God made. They had two sons. They were the first family.**
6. Have the children open the flaps and draw a picture of their own families inside.
7. When the pictures are finished, have the children show the pictures of their families. Practice the memory verse together. Ask, **Can you point to Adam and Eve? Where are their sons? This is the first family God made.**

EXTRA TIME

Provide magazine cut-outs of families. Have the children glue one or more of the cut-outs inside the folding picture.

Color a picture of the first family that God made. Then draw a picture of your own family.

The Lord God made a woman...

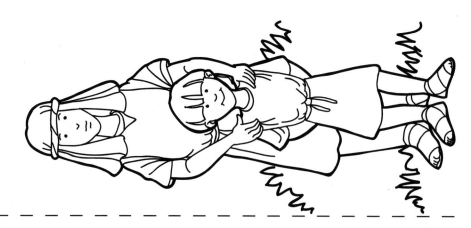

...and brought her to the man. Genesis 2:22

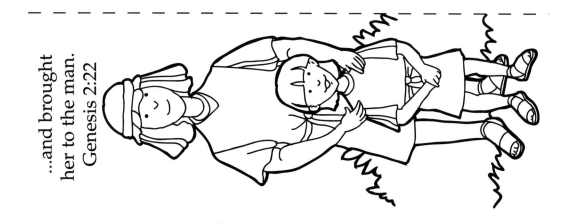

Noah Obeys God
Genesis Chapters 6-9

MEMORY VERSE

Take…two of every kind of…animal.
~ Genesis 7:2

WHAT YOU NEED

- page 14, duplicated
- crayons
- safety scissors
- yarn
- tape

BEFORE CLASS

Duplicate a pattern page for each child. For younger children, cut the four sections apart. Cut a one-yard length of yarn for each child. Make a sample to show the children.

WHAT TO DO

1. Introduce the lesson by telling the story of Noah's ark from Genesis chapters 6-9. Say, **God told Noah to build a great big boat called an ark. Then God told Noah to bring the mommy and daddy of each animal onto the ark. Noah gathered two of each kind of animal into the ark to stay safe from the big flood.**
2. Show the children the sample craft.
3. Distribute a pattern page to each child.
4. Say the memory verse.
5. Help the children cut the page into the four sections, then fold on the broken lines.
6. Have the children color the animals.
7. Tape the length of yarn inside the fold of each animal section.
8. When the marching animals are finished, mark off an area of the room with tape. Say, **Here is an ark. Let's bring our animals into the ark.** Have the children take turns pulling their animals by the yarn along the floor and into the ark.

EXTRA TIME

Provide yarn for tails, cotton for fur and small feathers for birds. Have the children glue the textured items onto the animals.

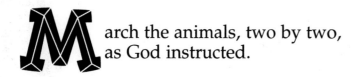 arch the animals, two by two, as God instructed.

Take...two of every kind of...animal.
Genesis 7:2

Abraham & Sarah Have a Son

Genesis 21:1-7; Genesis 7:15-18

MEMORY VERSE	
The Lord did...what he had promised. ~ Genesis 21:1	The Lord did...

what he had promised.
Genesis 21:1

WHAT YOU NEED

- page 16, duplicated
- crayons
- safety scissors
- glue

BEFORE CLASS

Duplicate a pattern page for each child. For younger children, cut out the two sticker squares. Make a sample to show the children.

WHAT TO DO

1. Introduce the lesson by telling the story from Genesis 21:1-7. Say, **Abraham and Sarah were very old. They both loved and obeyed God. What they wanted most was a child of their own. God told Abraham that Sarah would have a son. Abraham laughed because Sarah was so very old. But God kept His promise. Sarah soon had a son. His name was Isaac. God always keeps His promises.**
2. Show the children the sample.
3. Distribute a pattern page to each child.
4. Say the memory verse.
5. Have the children cut out the two sticker squares.
6. Help the children glue the sticker of Isaac at the bottom right-hand corner of the picture.
7. Help the children glue the verse sticker in the upper left-hand corner.
8. Use the leftover time for the children to color the picture.
9. When the pictures are finished, practice the verse together. Ask, **What did God promise to Abraham? How did God keep His promise?** Have the children point to the people in the picture as you retell the story.

EXTRA TIME

On the back of the picture, have the children draw a picture of a promise God has kept to them. Give suggestions to help them think of something to draw (food, care of family, Jesus and so on).

ake a sticker picture of Abraham,
Sarah and Isaac.

The Lord did... | **what he had promised.**
Genesis 21:1

A Servant Finds a Wife for Isaac
Genesis Chapter 24

MEMORY VERSE

Then the man bowed down and worshiped the Lord.
~ Genesis 24:26

WHAT YOU NEED

- page 18, duplicated
- crayons

BEFORE CLASS

Duplicate a pattern page for each child. Make a sample to show the children.

WHAT TO DO

1. Introduce the lesson by telling the Bible story from Genesis chapter 24. Say, **The servant asked God to help him know which woman would be Isaac's wife. Rebekah offered to give water to the animals. Then the servant knew she was God's answer to his prayer. God answered the servant's prayer and helped him find Rebekah to be Isaac's wife. God answers our prayers.**
2. Show younger children the sample. For older preschoolers, don't show the completed picture because they will enjoy discovering it as they connect the broken lines.
3. Distribute a pattern page to each child. Say the memory verse.
4. Have the children connect the dots to find for which animals Rebekah drew water. Then allow time for coloring the picture.
5. When the pictures are finished, practice the memory verse together. Ask, **To which animals did Rebekah give water? How did God answer the servant's prayer? Yes, God, helped the servant find Rebekah to be Isaac's wife.**

EXTRA TIME

Provide brown construction paper or brown paper bags. Have the children cut or tear small pieces of paper and glue it to the camels for texture.

ebekah offered to give water to the servant and to the animals. The servant's prayer was answered. Connect the dashed lines to find the animals to which Rebekah gave water.

Then the man bowed down
and worshiped the Lord.
Genesis 24:26

Joseph's New Coat
Genesis 37:2-4

MEMORY VERSE

[Jacob] loved Joseph...and he made a...robe for him.
~ Genesis 37:3

[Jacob] loved Joseph...and he made a...robe for him.
Genesis 37:3

WHAT YOU NEED

- page 20, duplicated
- crayons
- brightly-colored construction paper
- scissors or craft knife
- tape
- glue (optional)

BEFORE CLASS

Duplicate a pattern page for each child. Use a craft knife or scissors to cut the slits in the pictures. Cut two 1" x 8" strips of bright construction paper for each child. Make a sample craft to show the children.

WHAT TO DO

1. Introduce the lesson by telling Joseph's story from Genesis 37:2-4.
2. Say, **Jacob loved Joseph very much. He gave Joseph a beautiful coat of many colors to show his love. Families do special things to show they love each other.**
3. Show the children the sample craft.
4. Distribute a pattern page to each child.
5. Say the memory verse.
6. Have the children weave the strips through the slits in the picture. (Have younger preschoolers simply glue the strips onto the picture.)
7. Tape the ends at the back of the picture.
8. Have the children color the picture. Say, **Your family loves you, too. Can you say some things your parents do to show they love you?** Allow time for the children to respond.

EXTRA TIME

For a more challenging activity, make the strips ½-inch wide and 5 inches long. Cut five colors of strips for each child. Cut slits at the sides of the robe in five places and have the children weave the strips across the robe.

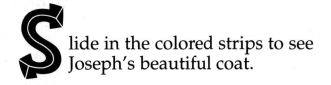 

Slide in the colored strips to see Joseph's beautiful coat.

[Jacob] loved Joseph…and he made a…robe for him.
Genesis 37:3

Joseph Saves His Brothers
Genesis chapters 42-45

MEMORY VERSE

God sent me...to save your lives.
~ Genesis 45:7

God sent me...to save your lives.
Genesis 45:7

WHAT YOU NEED

- page 22, duplicated
- crayons

BEFORE CLASS

Duplicate a pattern page for each child. Make a sample craft to show the children.

WHAT TO DO

1. Introduce the lesson by telling the story of Joseph saving his family, found in Genesis chapters 42-45. Say, **God had a plan for Joseph's life. God has a plan for your life, too.**
2. Show the children the sample craft.
3. Distribute a pattern page to each child.
4. Say the memory verse.
5. Have the children trace the broken lines to write GOD.
6. Ask, **Who had a plan for Joseph's life? Yes, it was God.** Discuss plans God may have for each child's life.
7. Have the children color the picture.

EXTRA TIME

Have the children turn the picture to the back. Say, **Draw a picture of a plan you think God has for your life.** (For example: preacher, singer, teacher, etc.)

Color the picture and trace the word
to find out who sent Joseph to
save his brothers.

God sent me...to save your lives.
Genesis 45:7

Moses Is Born
Exodus 2:1-10

MEMORY VERSE

She named him Moses.
~ Exodus 2:10

1. Moses' mother made a basket.

daughter found n the basket.

WHAT YOU NEED

- page 24, duplicated
- crayons
- safety scissors
- tape

BEFORE CLASS

Duplicate a pattern page for each child. For younger children, cut the page in half on the solid line and tape it at the marked edges. Make a sample craft to show the children.

WHAT TO DO

1. Introduce the lesson by telling the story of Moses' birth from Exodus 2:1-10. Say, **God helped baby Moses' mother find a way to keep him safe. God took care of Moses. God will take care of you, too.**
2. Show the children the sample craft.
3. Distribute a pattern page to each child.
4. Say the memory verse.
5. Have the children cut the page on the solid line, then tape it at the edges to connect pages 2 and 3.
6. Have the children fold the booklet on the broken lines, and color the pictures (page one should be on top). Have the children "read" their books and point to the pictures as you retell the story.

EXTRA TIME

Have the children draw their own version of the story on the back of the booklet pages. Or, have the children draw their version of another part of the story of Moses.

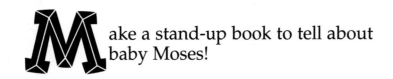

ake a stand-up book to tell about
baby Moses!

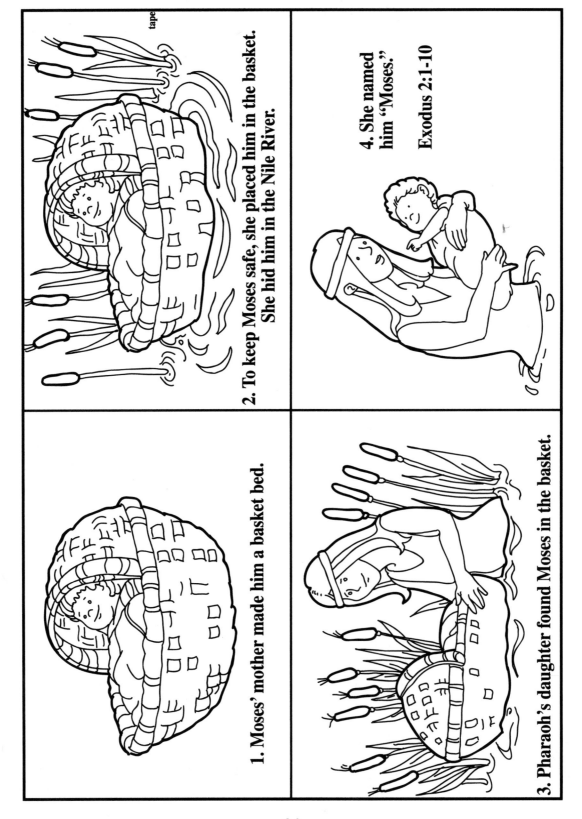

tape

2. To keep Moses safe, she placed him in the basket.
She hid him in the Nile River.

4. She named
him "Moses."

Exodus 2:1-10

1. Moses' mother made him a basket bed.

3. Pharaoh's daughter found Moses in the basket.

God Speaks to Moses
Exodus Chapter 3

MEMORY VERSE

Moses saw that though the bush was on fire it did not burn up.
~ Exodus 3:2

WHAT YOU NEED

- page 26, duplicated
- crayons
- safety scissors
- tape

BEFORE CLASS

Duplicate a pattern page for each child. For younger children, cut the strip from the page and tape it onto the right edge of picture. Make a sample craft to show the children.

WHAT TO DO

1. Introduce the lesson by telling the story of Moses and the burning bush from Exodus chapter 3. Say, **Moses knew something special was happening when he saw the bush was on fire but didn't burn. Then God spoke to Moses. God speaks to us today through His Word, the Bible.**
2. Show the children the sample craft.
3. Distribute a pattern page to each child.
4. Say the memory verse.
5. Have the children cut the strip from the page and tape it to the right edge of picture.
6. Have the children color the picture. Discuss some things God tells us through His Word (He loves us, He wants us to obey, He wants us to worship Him, etc.).
7. Have children retell the story, using the folding picture flaps.

EXTRA TIME

Provide red and green tissue paper. Have the children crumple bits of paper. Show how to glue red tissue paper to the burning bush and green tissue to the regular bush.

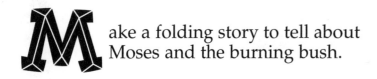

Make a folding story to tell about Moses and the burning bush.

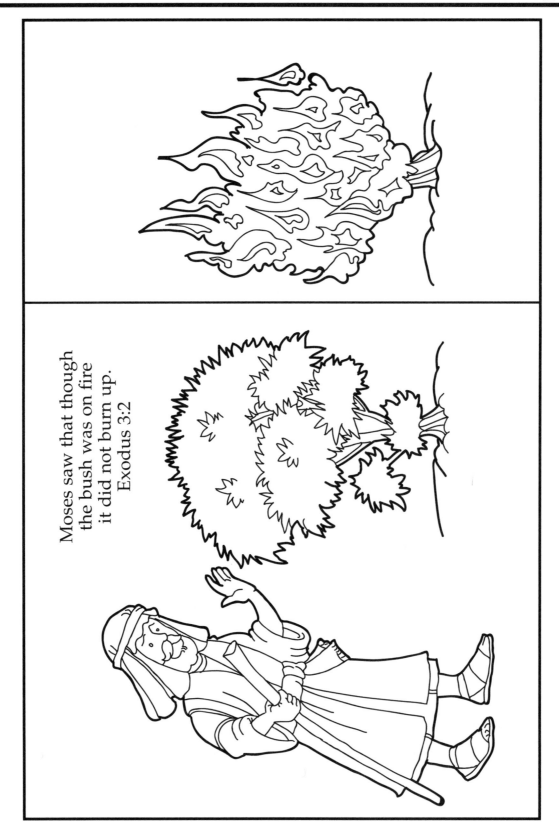

Moses saw that though the bush was on fire it did not burn up. Exodus 3:2

Crossing the Red Sea
Exodus 13:17-14:31

MEMORY VERSE

The Lord saved Israel.
~ Exodus 14:30

The Lord saved Israel.
Exodus 14:30

WHAT YOU NEED

- page 28, duplicated
- crayons
- yarn
- tape

BEFORE CLASS

Duplicate a pattern page for each child. Cut one 2-foot length of yarn per child. Make a sample craft to show the children.

WHAT TO DO

1. Introduce the lesson by telling the story of the Israelites crossing the Red Sea from Exodus 13:17-14:31. Say, **God made the land dry so His people could cross the Red Sea. God helps His people.**
2. Show the children the sample craft.
3. Distribute a pattern page to each child.
4. Say the memory verse.
5. Have the children fold the page in half on the dashed line.
6. Show how to tape the yarn to the front end of the pull toy.
7. Have the children color the pictures on both sides of the Israelites.
8. Encourage the children to pull their toys as you tell the story of the Israelites crossing the Red Sea again.

EXTRA TIME

Use the pull toys to have fun races. Line the children up and have them race their pull toys across a marked area.

 ake a toy to pretend you are crossing the Red Sea with Moses and the Israelites.

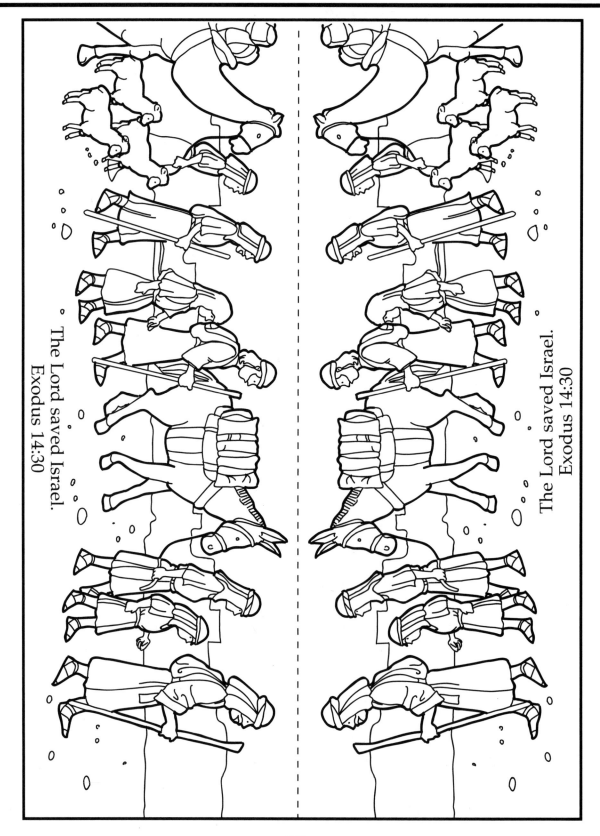

The Lord saved Israel.
Exodus 14:30

The Lord saved Israel.
Exodus 14:30

Moses on the Mountain
Exodus Chapters 19-20

MEMORY VERSE

I am the Lord your God.
~ Exodus 20:2

WHAT YOU NEED

- page 30, duplicated
- crayons
- safety scissors

I am the Lord your God.
Exodus 20:2

BEFORE CLASS

Duplicate a pattern page for each child. For younger children, cut the page on the bold line. Make a sample craft to show the children.

WHAT TO DO

1. Introduce the lesson by telling about Moses meeting on the mountain with God, from Exodus chapters 19-20.
2. Say, **Moses climbed the mountain to meet with God. God gave Moses some rules for His people. God's Word, the Bible, tells us the rules God wants us to follow. These are the same rules God gave Moses on the mountain.**
3. Show the children the sample craft.
4. Distribute a pattern page to each child.
5. Say the memory verse.
6. Have the children cut the pattern on the bold line, being careful not to cut the dashed lines (you will need to start their cuts for them).
7. Show how to fold the remainder of page on the dashed lines to form a stand-up picture.
8. Allow the children to color the picture. Read the commandments from Exodus 20:3-17 using words the children can understand easily.

EXTRA TIME

For older preschoolers, provide bark, leaves and pebbles for them to glue on to the picture.

ake a stand-up picture that shows Moses on the mountain with the rules from God.

I am the Lord your God.
Exodus 20:2

Ruth Stays with Naomi
Book of Ruth

MEMORY VERSE

Where you go I will go.
~ Ruth 1:16

1= blue
2= yellow
3= brown

Where you go I will go.
Ruth 1:16

WHAT YOU NEED

- page 32, duplicated
- crayons (yellow, blue and brown)

BEFORE CLASS

Duplicate a pattern page for each child. Make a sample craft to show the children.

WHAT TO DO

1. Introduce the lesson by telling the story of Ruth and Naomi. Say, **Ruth loved Naomi very much. She said, "I will always stay with you." Ruth promised to stay with Naomi and help her. She promised to worship God, too. We can promise to worship God.**
2. Show the children the sample craft.
3. Distribute a pattern page to each child.
4. Say the memory verse.
5. Have the children put a mark by each number at the top of page to show which color to use for that number. Then allow time for children to color the picture by number. (Various shades of these colors will work in order to have enough of each to go around.)
6. Discuss ways in which we can worship God.

EXTRA TIME

Cut a slit at each corner as shown. Fold the page to form a self-frame. Tape the corners to hold the frame shape.

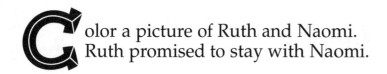 olor a picture of Ruth and Naomi.
Ruth promised to stay with Naomi.

1= blue
2= yellow
3= brown

Where you go I will go.
Ruth 1:16

Samuel Serves God
1 Samuel Chapter 1

MEMORY VERSE

So now I give him to the Lord.
~ 1 Samuel 1:28

WHAT YOU NEED

- page 34, duplicated
- crayons

BEFORE CLASS

Duplicate a pattern page for each child. Make a sample craft to show the children.

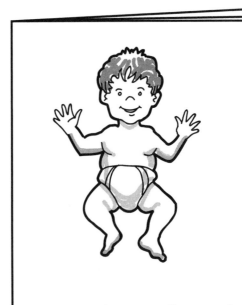

A Book About Samuel

WHAT TO DO

1. Tell the story of Samuel's birth and Hannah's promise to God from 1 Samuel, chapter 1. Say, **Hannah asked God for a son. She promised to give her son to serve God all his life. God gave Hannah a son, and she kept her promise to God. Samuel served God all his life. Even when he was a child, Samuel served God. We can all serve God.**
2. Show the children the sample craft.
3. Distribute a pattern page to each child.
4. Say the memory verse.
5. Help the children fold the page into quarters to form a booklet.
6. Have the children color the pages. Discuss some ways Samuel may have helped Eli in the temple. Then discuss ways the children can serve God.

EXTRA TIME

Read each page to the children as they work. Prepare the children to be able to retell the story of Samuel to someone at home. Also, consider having the children help with a church project such as cleaning the nursery, picking up papers in the sanctuary after the service or handing out bulletins.

M ake a book that tells how Samuel was dedicated to God.

A Book About Samuel

Hannah kept her promise. She took Samuel to live at the temple with Eli.

Hannah asked God for a son. She promised to give the son to serve God all his life.

God gave Hannah a son.

David and Goliath
1 Samuel Chapter 17

> ### MEMORY VERSE
>
> *I come...in the name of the Lord.*
> ~ 1 Samuel 17:45

WHAT YOU NEED

- page 36, duplicated
- crayons
- safety scissors
- letter-size envelopes

BEFORE CLASS

Duplicate a pattern page for each child. For younger children, cut the page into the four marked pieces. Make a sample craft to show the children.

WHAT TO DO

1. Introduce the lesson by telling the story of David and Goliath from 1 Samuel, chapter 17. Say, **David was not afraid of Goliath. Do you know why? Because David knew God was with him. Listen to what David said to Goliath: "I come in the name of the Lord." We can do anything with God's help, too.**
2. Show the children the sample craft.
3. Distribute a pattern page to each child.
4. Say the memory verse.
5. Have the children color the page.
6. Show how to cut the page into the four marked pieces.
7. Distribute a letter-size envelope to each child for storing the pieces.
8. Discuss times the children may be afraid, such as telling others about God. Say, **God will help you. You can do great things in the name of the Lord.**

EXTRA TIME

Allow time for the children to work their puzzles before dismissal. Encourage the children to retell the Bible story in their own words.

ake a puzzle about David battling the giant Goliath. Find out what David said to Goliath.

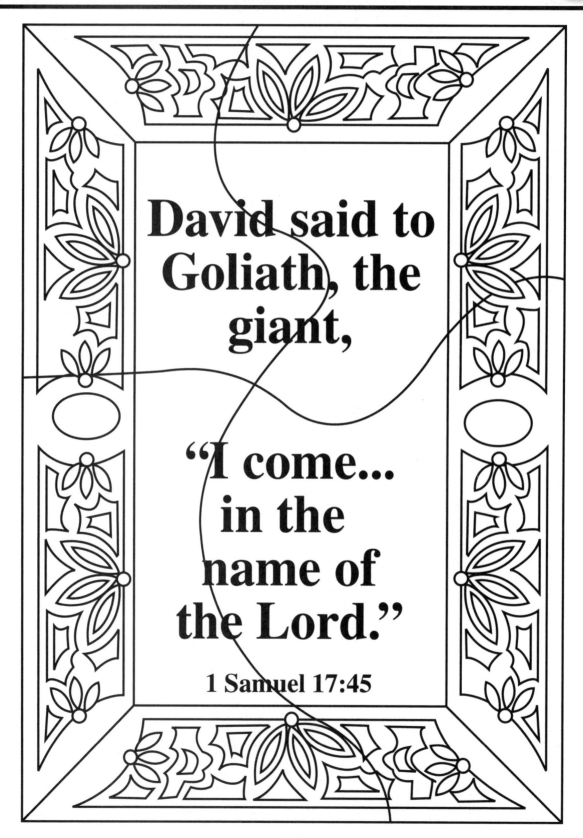

David said to Goliath, the giant,

"I come... in the name of the Lord."

1 Samuel 17:45

David and Jonathan
1 Samuel Chapter 20

MEMORY VERSE

We have sworn friendship with each other in the name of the Lord.
~ 1 Samuel 20:42

WHAT YOU NEED

- page 38, duplicated
- crayons

BEFORE CLASS

Duplicate a pattern page for each child. Make a sample craft to show the children.

WHAT TO DO

1. Tell the story of David and Jonathan's friendship from 1 Samuel, chapter 20. Say, **David and Jonathan were very good friends. They were friends in the Lord. We are all special friends in the Lord.** Name each child and say, **[Name] is my friend. We are all friends in the Lord.**
2. Show the children the sample craft.
3. Distribute a pattern page to each child.
4. Say the memory verse.
5. Have the children connect the dots to find Jonathan, David's friend. Ask, **Who did you find in the dot-to-dot picture? Yes, it's Jonathan, David's friend. It's fun to have friends in the Lord.**
6. Allow the children to color the picture.

EXTRA TIME

To make easy friendship bracelets, cut 2" x 8" strips of paper. Have the children copy the phrase "Friends in the Lord" on two strips (one for the child and another for a friend). Help the children tape on their bracelets.

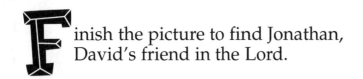

Finish the picture to find Jonathan,
David's friend in the Lord.

David and Jonathan are friends in the Lord.

We have sworn friendship with each other in the name of the Lord.
1 Samuel 20:42

Solomon Builds God's Temple
1 Kings Chapters 6-8

WHAT YOU NEED

- page 40, duplicated
- construction paper
- crayons
- safety scissors
- glue

BEFORE CLASS

Duplicate a pattern page for each child. For younger children, cut out the four puzzle pieces. Make a sample craft to show the children.

WHAT TO DO

1. Introduce the lesson by telling the children about the beautiful temple that was built. Say, **Solomon made sure that God's house was made from the best materials. He saw that God's house was built just the way God wanted it. God wants us to take care of His house. We go to God's house to worship.**
2. Show the children the sample craft.
3. Distribute a pattern page to each child.
4. Say the memory verse.
5. Allow the children to color the puzzle in beautiful colors (offer metallic crayons, if available).
6. Have the children cut out the four puzzle pieces.
7. Help the students arrange the pieces in order on a sheet of construction paper.
8. Help the children glue the pieces onto the construction paper. Say, **Solomon built a beautiful temple for God. We can keep God's house beautiful, too.** Discuss ways we can help to take care of God's house.

EXTRA TIME

Provide gold glitter to sprinkle on the temple. For older preschoolers, cut the puzzle into more pieces for increased difficulty. Or, have the children draw a picture of your church and cut the picture into puzzle pieces.

ut together a poster to show the beautiful temple that Solomon built for God.

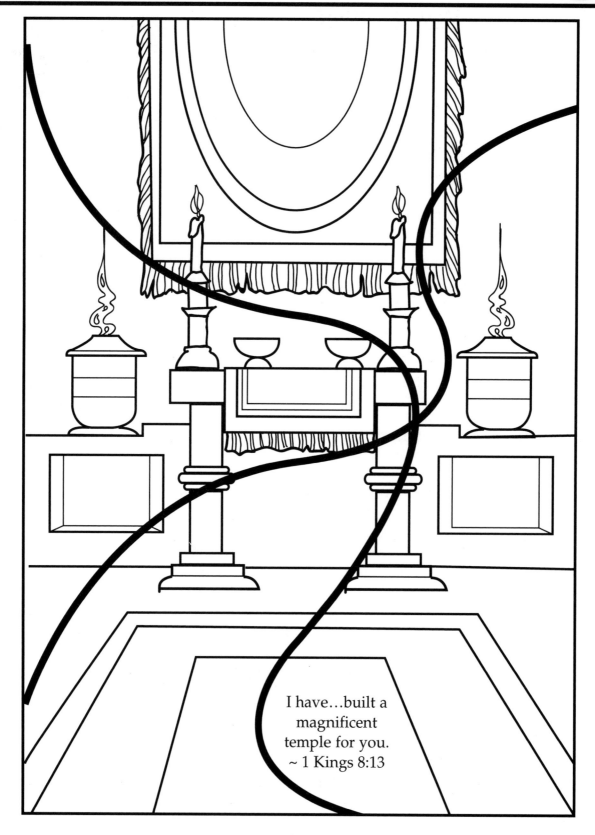

I have...built a magnificent temple for you.
~ 1 Kings 8:13

God Takes Care of Elijah

1 Kings 17:1-6

MEMORY VERSE

He did what the Lord had told him.
~ 1 Kings 17:5

WHAT YOU NEED

- page 42, duplicated
- crayons
- glue
- small crackers

BEFORE CLASS

Duplicate a pattern page for each child. Make a sample craft to show the children.

He did what the Lord
had told him.
1 Kings 17:5

WHAT TO DO

1. Introduce the lesson by telling the story from 1 Kings 17:1-6. Say, **God took good care of Elijah. He had Elijah stay beside a stream with plenty of water. God sent ravens to feed Elijah bread and meat. God takes good care of us, too.**
2. Show the children the sample craft.
3. Distribute a pattern page to each child.
4. Say the memory verse.
5. Have the children glue some crackers in the birds' beaks, then color the picture.
6. Have the children use their pictures to retell the story. Ask, **How did God get meat and bread to Elijah? Yes, He sent ravens to bring the food to Elijah.**

EXTRA TIME

Provide feathers or black tissue paper to glue onto the ravens. Have the children retell the story in their own words.

od took care of Elijah by providing water, bread and meat. Make a picture to show others how well God took care of Elijah.

Ravens brought Elijah food.

He did what the Lord had told him.
1 Kings 17:5

The Widow's Oil
2 Kings 4:1-7

MEMORY VERSE

He provides.
~ Psalm 111:5

WHAT YOU NEED

- page 44, duplicated
- crayons

BEFORE CLASS

Duplicate a pattern page for each child. Make a sample craft to show the children. (Do not complete the entire craft for older children. They will enjoy looking for the jars themselves.)

WHAT TO DO

1. Introduce the lesson by telling the story from 2 Kings 4:1-7. Say, **God helped Elisha take care of the widow and her two sons. God always takes care of us.**
2. Show the children the sample craft.
3. Distribute a pattern page to each child.
4. Say the memory verse.
5. Have the children find and circle the 10 jars.
6. Allow the children to color the picture. Ask, **What did Elisha tell the boys to find? Yes, empty jars. What was the woman able to pour into the jars? Yes, oil. Then they sold the oil so they could pay the money they owed and have money left to buy food and things they needed.**

EXTRA TIME

Have the children color the entire picture. Then help them put a few drops of cooking oil on a cotton ball and rub it on the picture. The oil will change the look of the picture, and give the children a closer feel for what was in the jars.

od helped Elijah take care of a widow's family. Find the jars in the picture to remember that God filled the jars with oil to help the widow.

He provides.
Psalm 111:5

Naaman Is Healed
2 Kings 5:1-14

MEMORY VERSE

He went down and dipped himself in the Jordan seven times.
~ 2 Kings 5:14

WHAT YOU NEED

- page 46, duplicated
- crayons
- tape

BEFORE CLASS

Duplicate a pattern page for each child. Make a sample craft to show the children.

WHAT TO DO

1. Introduce the lesson by telling the story of Naaman's healing from 2 Kings 5:1-14. Say, **Elisha told Naaman how to be healed from leprosy. At first, Naaman did not want to obey God. But when Naaman did obey God, the leprosy was gone. When we obey God, He will take care of us.**
2. Show the children the sample craft.
3. Distribute a pattern page to each child.
4. Say the memory verse.
5. Help the children fold the puppet on the dashed lines.
6. Show how to tape the puppet at the top and side, leaving the bottom edge open.
7. Have the children color their puppets.
8. Encourage the children to slip the puppets on their hands and hold up the puppets as they help you retell the story.

EXTRA TIME

Have the children act out the story using their puppets. Encourage them to retell the story in their own words.

U se the puppet to act out the story of how Naaman was healed from leprosy. Naaman obeyed God.

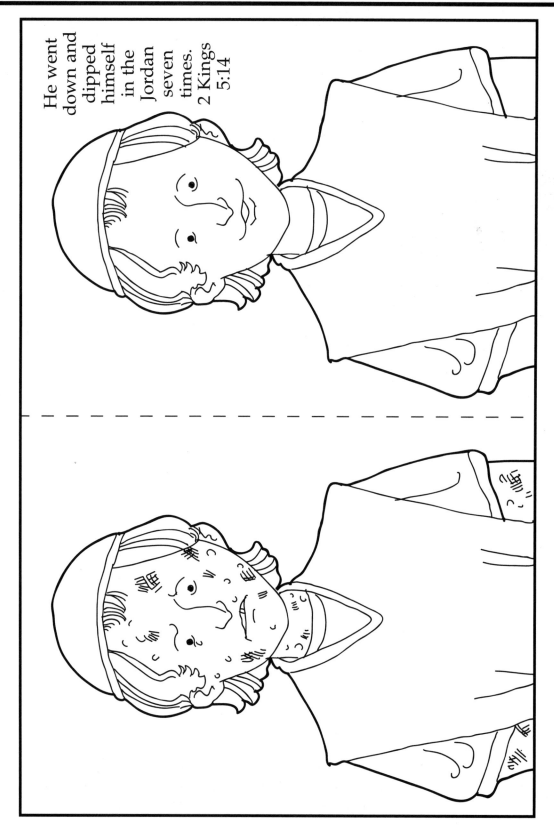

He went down and dipped himself in the Jordan seven times. 2 Kings 5:14

The Book of Law Is Found
2 Kings, Chapter 22

MEMORY VERSE

I have found the Book of Law in the temple of the Lord.
~ 2 Kings 22:8

WHAT YOU NEED

- page 48, duplicated
- crayons
- safety scissors
- tape
- plastic drinking straws
- yarn

BEFORE CLASS

Duplicate a pattern page and cut a 6-inch length of yarn for each child. For younger children, cut the page in half and tape it together in the center. You may want to tape the straws on each end before class, too. Make a sample craft to show the children.

WHAT TO DO

1. Introduce the lesson by telling the story from 2 Kings, chapter 22. Say, **The Book of Law was read to King Josiah. The king was sad that his people had sinned against God. We are happy when we learn God's Word. God wants us to obey His Word.**
2. Show the children the sample craft.
3. Distribute a pattern page to each child.
4. Say the memory verse.
5. Have the children cut the page in half and tape it together to form a long story strip.
6. Allow the children to color the story, then show how to tape a straw to each end of the story strip and roll each end halfway to the center.
7. Go around and tie the yarn around the scroll to hold it closed.
8. Read each section to the children as they color the story strip. When the scrolls are finished, show the children how to unroll a portion of the scroll and retell the story in their own words.

EXTRA TIME

Give each child a sheet of plain paper and black construction paper. Help them tape the plain paper to the black paper and fold it in half with the black paper on the outside. Have the children draw a picture of themselves obeying God on the inside.

ake a Bible times scroll that tells the story about King Josiah and God's law.

I have found the Book of Law in the temple of the Lord.
2 Kings 22:8

Job Praises God
Job, Chapters 1, 2 and 42

MEMORY VERSE

Job...was blameless.
~ Job 1:1

WHAT YOU NEED

- page 50, duplicated
- heavy white paper or card stock
- crayons
- safety scissors
- tape
- plastic drinking straws

BEFORE CLASS

Duplicate the pattern page onto heavy white paper or card stock for each child. You will need six straws per child. For younger children, you may want to cut out the puppet shapes. Make a sample craft to show the children.

WHAT TO DO

1. Introduce the lesson by telling the story of Job. Say, **Even when Job had lost everything, and even when Job was very sick, he still praised God. We can praise God at all times. Even if we are sick or sad, we can praise God.**
2. Show the children the sample craft.
3. Distribute a pattern page to each child.
4. Say the memory verse.
5. Have the children color and cut out the puppets.
6. Show how to tape a straw to the back of each puppet. Have the children use their puppets to act out the story of Job. Say, **Job praised God even when he was sad and sick. God blessed Job.**

EXTRA TIME

Give each child a paper plate. Help the children draw a happy face on their plate. Then say some situations, such as, "You are sick" or "You lost your dog" or "Your favorite toy is broken," etc. Prompt the children to hold up their happy faces and shout, "We praise God" after each phrase.

ake puppets to act out the story of Job. Remember that Job continued to praise God, even when he had troubles.

Job Job…was blameless. ~ Job 1:1

Mrs. Job

Eliphaz

Bildad

Zophar

Elihu

God Saves Daniel
Daniel Chapter 6

MEMORY VERSE

My God sent his angel, and he shut the mouths of the lions.
~ Daniel 6:22

WHAT YOU NEED

- page 52, duplicated
- crayons
- safety scissors

BEFORE CLASS

Duplicate a pattern page onto heavy white paper or card stock for each child. For younger children, cut out the lion and Daniel figures. Make a sample craft to show the children.

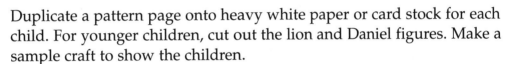

WHAT TO DO

1. Introduce the lesson by telling the story of Daniel in the lions' den from Daniel chapter 6. Say, **Daniel prayed to God even when he knew he could get thrown into the lions' den. When the king threw Daniel into the lions' den, the king said to Daniel, "I hope your God rescues you from the lions!" And God did! God helps us to do the right thing and be safe.**
2. Show the children the sample craft.
3. Distribute a pattern page to each child.
4. Say the memory verse.
5. Help the children cut out the lion and Daniel figures.
6. After the children color the figures, help to fold them on the dashed lines so they stand.
7. Encourage the children to act out the story using their play sets.

EXTRA TIME

Play Lion Tag. Choose one child to be the lion. Have the children play a traditional game of Tag. When a child is tagged, that child must fold his or hands in prayer to be saved from the lion. Change lions several times during the game.

ake a stand-up lion and Daniel.
Use the figures to tell how God
saved Daniel from the lions.

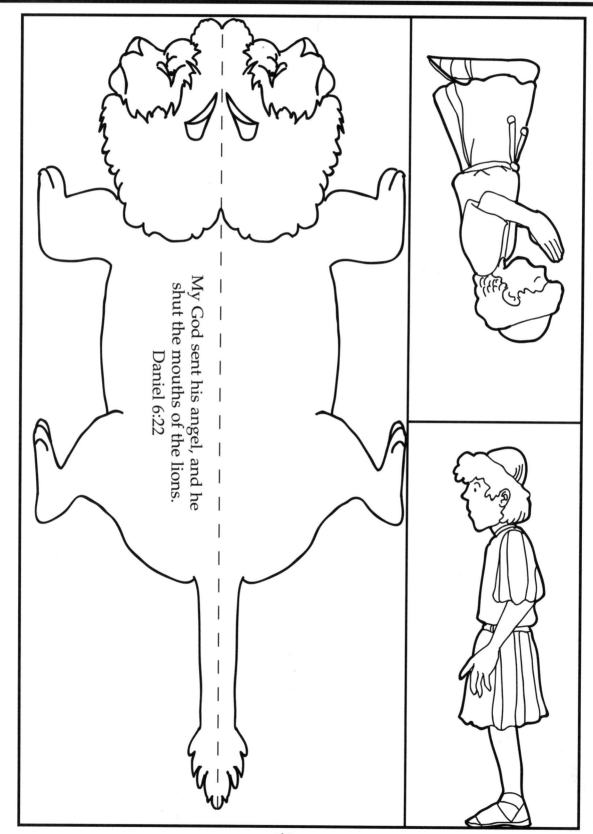

My God sent his angel, and he
shut the mouths of the lions.
Daniel 6:22

Jonah Runs from God
Jonah, Chapters 1-2

MEMORY VERSE

Jonah was inside the fish three days and three nights.
~ Jonah 1:17

WHAT YOU NEED

- page 54, duplicated
- crayons
- safety scissors
- glue
- 9" paper plates
- yarn
- hole punch

BEFORE CLASS

Duplicate a pattern page and cut an 8" length of yarn for each child. For younger children, cut out the two circle halves and Jonah. You also may want to fold and punch the plates. Make a sample craft to show the children.

WHAT TO DO

1. Introduce the lesson by telling the story of Jonah and the big fish from Jonah chapters 1-2. Say, **Jonah ran from God. When the big storm came, Jonah told the sailors to throw him into the sea. But God sent a big fish to swallow Jonah and save him from drowning. God always takes care of us.**
2. Show the children the sample craft.
3. Distribute a pattern page to each child. Say the memory verse.
4. Have the children cut out the two circle halves and Jonah.
5. Show how to fold a paper plate in half.
6. Help the children glue a circle half to each side of the plate on the outside and show where to glue Jonah inside the plate.
7. Go around and punch a hole in the top of the plate on each side.
8. Help the students thread yarn through the hole and tie it in a bow.
9. Have the children count to three. Say, Jonah was in the fish for three days and three nights. God took care of Jonah.

EXTRA TIME

Have the children color the edge of the plate and the inside as they wish. Encourage the children to retell the story in their own words.

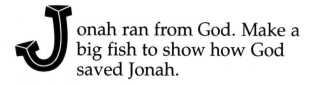 **J**onah ran from God. Make a
big fish to show how God
saved Jonah.

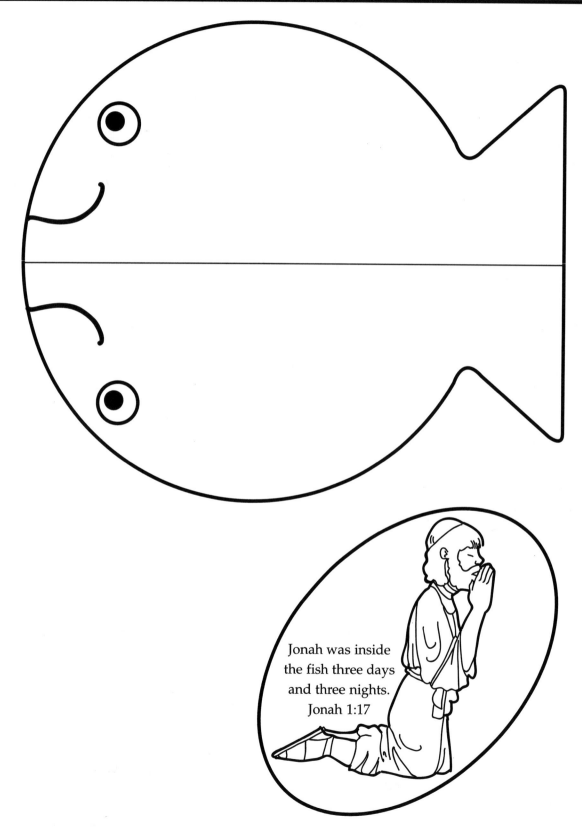

Jonah was inside
the fish three days
and three nights.
Jonah 1:17

An Angel Visits Mary
Luke 1:26-38

MEMORY VERSE

Nothing is impossible with God.
~ Luke 1:37

WHAT YOU NEED

- page 56, duplicated
- crayons
- safety scissors
- hole punch
- yarn
- coffee filters
- tape

BEFORE CLASS

Duplicate a pattern page and cut a 10-inch length of yarn for each child. For younger children, cut the page and the coffee filter in half. Make a sample craft to show the children.

WHAT TO DO

1. Introduce the lesson by telling the story of the angel and Mary from Luke 1:26-38. Say, **God sent an angel to tell Mary something very special. Mary was going to have a baby. His name was to be "Jesus." We are happy for the Good News the angel told Mary. We are happy that Jesus was born.**
2. Show the children the sample craft.
3. Distribute a pattern page to each child.
4. Say the memory verse.
5. Have the children cut the page and a coffee filter in half. Help them tape half of the filter on the inside of each side of the angel back.
6. Show where to tape the angel together at the top and sides.
7. Have the children color the angel.
8. Go around and punch a hole in the top of each angel figure. Thread the yarn through the hole and tie it for a hanger.
9. Have the children fold their hands and pray with you to thank God for baby Jesus.

EXTRA TIME

Have the children spread glue on the angel and wings, and sprinkle on some glitter.

Make an angel to remember that
God sent an angel to tell Mary the
good news.

Nothing is impossible
with God.
Luke 1:37

Jesus Is Born
Luke 2:1-7

MEMORY VERSE

Jesus was born in Bethlehem.
~ Matthew 2:1

WHAT YOU NEED

- page 58, duplicated
- crayons
- safety scissors
- glue

BEFORE CLASS

Duplicate a pattern page for each child. For younger children, cut the page apart on the solid line and cut out the three figures. Make a sample craft to show the children.

WHAT TO DO

1. Introduce the lesson by telling the story of Jesus' birth from Luke 2:1-7. Say, **God loves us and sent His Son, Jesus, for everyone.**
2. Show the children the sample craft.
3. Distribute a pattern page to each child.
4. Say the memory verse.
5. Allow the students to color the pictures.
6. Have the children cut out the stable scene and the three squares.
7. Help the children fold the stable scene on the dashed lines.
8. Have the students glue the pictures inside the stable, and the verse sticker on the outside, as shown.
9. Have the children point to the stickers on their picture and help you retell the story. Practice the memory verse together.

EXTRA TIME

Provide torn paper or straw for the children to glue on the floor of the stable.

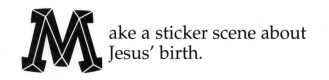 ake a sticker scene about
Jesus' birth.

Jesus was born
in Bethlehem.

Matthew 2:1

Bringing Good News
Luke 2:8-20

MEMORY VERSE

I bring you good news of great joy.
~ Luke 2:10

WHAT YOU NEED

- page 60, duplicated
- crayons
- safety scissors

BEFORE CLASS

Duplicate a pattern page for each child. For younger children, cut out the stand-up scene on the bold line. Make a sample craft to show the children.

WHAT TO DO

1. Introduce the lesson by telling the story from Luke 2:8-20. Say, **An angel told the shepherds that Jesus was born. Then many angels appeared and sang praises to God. We praise God, too, for baby Jesus. Thank You, God, for baby Jesus.**
2. Show the children the sample craft.
3. Distribute a pattern page to each child.
4. Say the memory verse.
5. Have the children cut on the bold line (you may need to start the cut for them).
6. Show how to fold the top of the page back on the fold lines so the scene stands.
7. Have the children color the scene. While the children stand up their angel scenes, lead the class in singing the memory verse to the tune of "Mary Had a Little Lamb."
   I bring you Good News of great joy, of great joy, of great joy!
   I bring you Good News of great joy. It's Good News of great joy.

EXTRA TIME

Allow the children to glue gold glitter onto the angel and a cotton ball on each sheep.

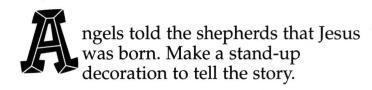 ngels told the shepherds that Jesus was born. Make a stand-up decoration to tell the story.

I bring you good news of great joy.
Luke 2:10

Wise Men Worship Jesus
Matthew 2:1-12

MEMORY VERSE

We saw his star in the east and have come to worship him.
~ Matthew 2:2

WHAT YOU NEED

- page 62, duplicated
- crayons
- glue
- glitter

BEFORE CLASS

Duplicate a pattern page for each child. Make a sample craft to show the children.

WHAT TO DO

1. Introduce the lesson by telling the story from Matthew 2:1-12. Say, **The wise men searched for baby Jesus. They followed the star to find Him. We are happy, too, that Jesus was born. We can worship Jesus like the wise men did.**
2. Show the children the sample craft.
3. Distribute a pattern page to each child.
4. Say the memory verse.
5. Have the children spread glue around the edge of the star, then sprinkle on glitter.
6. Allow the students to color the picture.
7. Read each section of the poster before the children color. Prepare the children to be able to retell the story at home.

EXTRA TIME

Cut out at least one small star shape from construction paper for each child. Let the children add stickers of baby Jesus to the stars. Add a length of yarn for a hanger. Say, **We can hang our stars on our Christmas trees at home to remember to worship Jesus.**

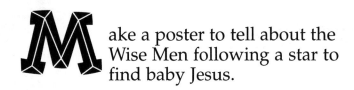 ake a poster to tell about the Wise Men following a star to find baby Jesus.

The Wise Men traveled to Jerusalem to find baby Jesus.

The Wise Men followed a star.

The star stopped over the house where Jesus was with His parents.

The Wise Men gave Jesus gifts.

John the Baptist Is Born
Luke 1:5-25; 57-80

MEMORY VERSE

He will be great in the sight of the Lord.
~ Luke 1:15

WHAT YOU NEED
- page 64, duplicated
- crayons
- safety scissors
- tape

BEFORE CLASS
Duplicate a pattern page for each child. For younger children, cut the strip from the page and cut the hole for Zechariah's mouth. Make a sample craft to show the children.

WHAT TO DO
1. Introduce the lesson by telling the story from Luke 1:5-25 and 57-80. Say, **Zechariah learned that God keeps His promises. Zechariah was happy baby John was born.**
2. Show the children the sample craft.
3. Distribute a pattern page to each child.
4. Say the memory verse.
5. Have the children cut the strip from the page and cut the mouth section from the puppet.
6. Show how to fold the page in half to form the puppet. Tape the side only.
7. Have the children color the puppet.
8. Show how to place the strip inside the puppet, so that the mouths show through the hole in the puppet. Add more tape around the edges as needed to keep the strip from moving from side to side.
9. Retell the story, having the children open and close Zechariah's mouth as the story says.

EXTRA TIME
Play a game. Find a picture of an angel to use. Have the children sing some simple songs. Now and then, hold up the angel. Instruct the children to close their mouths when they see the angel. Say, **When Zechariah didn't believe the angel, he wasn't able to talk.**

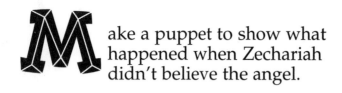ake a puppet to show what happened when Zechariah didn't believe the angel.

An angel appeared to Zechariah in the temple, and said, "Your prayer has been heard. Your wife Elizabeth will have a son, and you are to call him John."

Zechariah asked how his wife could have a baby, since they were both so old. The angel said, I have been sent from God to tell you this good news. But since you do not believe me, you will not be able to speak until the child is born.

Zechariah was not able to speak.

Soon, Elizabeth had a baby boy. Many people told them names for the baby. But, Elizabeth said, "His name is John."

Right then, Zechariah was able to speak. He began to praise God!

(Luke 5:2-25 and 57-80)

Jesus in His Father's House
Luke 2:41-52

MEMORY VERSE

I had to be in my Father's house.
~ Luke 2:49

WHAT YOU NEED

- page 66, duplicated
- crayons

BEFORE CLASS

Duplicate a pattern page for each child. Make a sample craft to show the children.

WHAT TO DO

1. Introduce the lesson by telling the story from Luke 2:41-52. Say, **Jesus loved God's House. We should love God's House, too.**
2. Show the children the sample craft.
3. Distribute a pattern page to each child.
4. Say the memory verse.
5. Help the children fold the page on the dashed lines as shown.
6. Have the children trace the picture of God's House in the center section. The children may color the page as they want. Ask, **What do you like to do best in God's House? What do you think Jesus liked to do in God's House?**

EXTRA TIME

Add texture to the picture by providing fabric scraps for the children to glue onto the clothing. Provide sand to glue on the picture of the church.

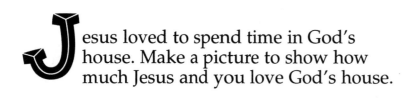

Jesus loved to spend time in God's house. Make a picture to show how much Jesus and you love God's house.

I had to be in my Father's house.

Luke 2:49

Jesus Is Baptized
Matthew 3:13-17

MEMORY VERSE

This is my Son, whom I love.
~ Matthew 3:17

WHAT YOU NEED

- page 68, duplicated
- crayons
- safety scissors

BEFORE CLASS

Duplicate a pattern page for each child. For younger children, cut the strip from the page and cut the slits above Jesus' head. Make a sample craft to show the children.

WHAT TO DO

1. Introduce the lesson by telling the story of Jesus' baptism from Matthew 3:13-17. Ask, **What came down from heaven? What did God's voice say? God wants us to know that Jesus is His Son.**
2. Show the children the sample craft.
3. Distribute a pattern page to each child.
4. Say the memory verse.
5. Have the children cut the strip from the page.
6. Help children cut the two slits above Jesus' head.
7. Show how to insert the strip through the slits. Show the children how to make the dove "descend" from heaven.
8. Have the children color the picture as they wish. Retell the story while the children make the dove "descend" from heaven.

EXTRA TIME

Provide blue watercolor paint, paintbrushes or cotton swabs and protective smocks. Allow time for the children to paint the water in the picture.

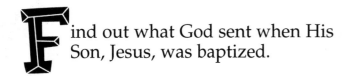 ind out what God sent when His Son, Jesus, was baptized.

This is my Son, whom I love.
Matthew 3:17

Jesus Calls Followers
Luke 5:1-11, 27-32; 6:12-16

MEMORY VERSE

"Follow me," Jesus said.
~ Luke 5:27

"Follow me," Jesus said.
Luke 5:27

WHAT YOU NEED

- page 70, duplicated
- crayons

BEFORE CLASS

Duplicate a pattern page for each child. Make a sample craft to show the children.

WHAT TO DO

1. Introduce the lesson by telling the story from Luke 5:1-11, 27-32; 6:12-16. Say the names of all the disciples. Say, **Jesus chose 12 special helpers. We can be Jesus' helpers, too. We can follow Jesus.**
2. Show the sample craft to the children.
3. Distribute a pattern page to each child.
4. Say the memory verse.
5. Have the children draw a happy smile on each face. Say the names of the 12 disciples as the children work.
6. Have the children color the poster. Say the name of each disciple, counting 1-12. Prepare the children to be able to say some of the names and know that there were 12 followers.

EXTRA TIME

Play the Helping Game. Have the children sing the following song while they help put away toys or classroom supplies. Sing to the tune of "Twinkle, Twinkle Little Star."
Jesus said, "Come follow Me."
Happy helpers you will be.
Helping me and others, too.
That's what God wants you to do.
Jesus said, "Come follow Me."
Happy helpers you will be.

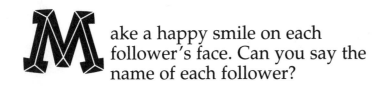 ake a happy smile on each follower's face. Can you say the name of each follower?

"Follow me," Jesus said.
Luke 5:27

Jesus Does Miracles
Luke 4:40-41

Jesus healed many.
~ Mark 1:34

WHAT YOU NEED

- page 72, duplicated
- crayons

BEFORE CLASS

Duplicate a pattern page for each child. Make a sample craft to show the children.

WHAT TO DO

1. Introduce the lesson by telling the story from Luke 4:40-41. Say, **Jesus made many people well. He did these miracles to show He was God.**
2. Show the children the sample craft.
3. Distribute a pattern page to each child.
4. Say the memory verse.
5. Have the children complete the picture by tracing the dashed lines. Tell about each miracle as the children work. Say, **Jesus did miracles to show He was God's Son.**

EXTRA TIME

Provide watercolor paint, cotton swabs or brushes and protective smocks. Have the children paint the picture.

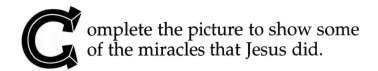 omplete the picture to show some of the miracles that Jesus did.

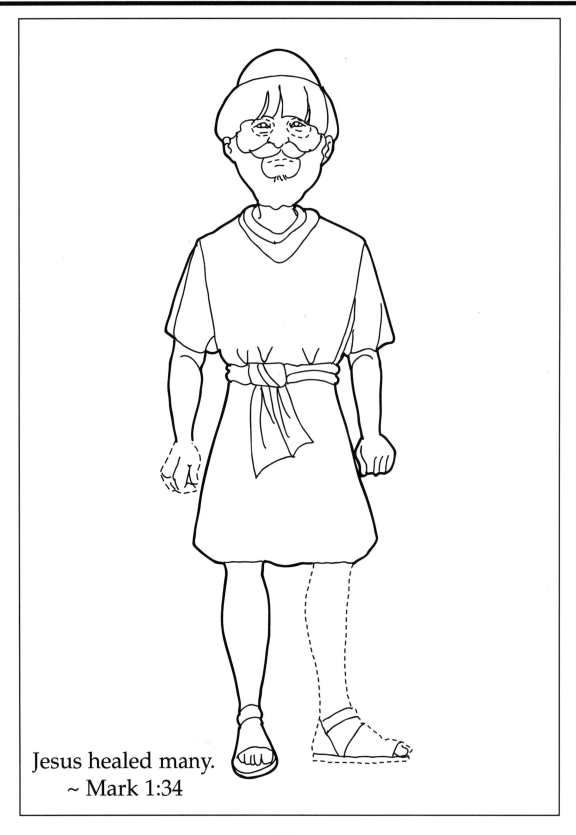

Jesus healed many.
~ Mark 1:34

Jesus Tells How to Be Happy
Matthew 5:1-12

WHAT YOU NEED

- page 74, duplicated
- crayons

BEFORE CLASS

Duplicate a pattern page for each child. Make a sample craft to show the children.

WHAT TO DO

1. Introduce the lesson by telling the story from Matthew 5:1-12. Say, **Jesus taught the people many things. He told them how to be happy. We, too, can learn how to be happy by following Jesus.**
2. Show the children the sample craft.
3. Distribute a pattern page to each child.
4. Say the memory verse.
5. Have the children fold the page into quarters.
6. Have the children color the booklet. Read the verses to the children as they work.
7. Encourage the children to act out each of the scenes from their booklets.

EXTRA TIME

Provide happy face stickers for the children to stick in their books. For low-cost stickers, trace a nickel onto paper. Cut out several layers at a time. Draw a happy face on each one, or let the children draw their own happy faces.

ake a booklet that tells how to be happy. These verses are called the Beatitudes.

Matthew 5:8

Blessed are the pure in heart, for they will see God.

Matthew 5:6

Blessed are those who hunger and thirst for righteousness, for they will be filled.

Blessed are the peacemakers, for they will be called sons of God.

Matthew 5:9

Jesus taught us how to be happy.

Jesus and the Children
Mark 10:13-16

MEMORY VERSE

Let the little children come to me.
~ Mark 10:14

WHAT YOU NEED

- page 76, duplicated
- crayons

BEFORE CLASS

Duplicate a pattern page for each child. Make a sample to show the children. Do not show the puzzle to older children, as they will enjoy figuring out the mazes themselves.

WHAT TO DO

1. Introduce the lesson by telling the story from Mark 10:13-16. Say, **Jesus loves little children. He told the other men, "Let the children come to me." Jesus loves little children just like you.**
2. Show the children the sample puzzle.
3. Distribute a puzzle to each child.
4. Say the memory verse.
5. Have the children follow the three mazes. Say, **These children in our picture are trying to find Jesus. The children loved Jesus and He loved them. Jesus loves you, too.**

EXTRA TIME

On the back of the page, have the children draw pictures of themselves with Jesus.

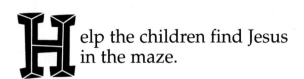

Help the children find Jesus in the maze.

Zacchaeus Knew Jesus
Luke 19:4-10

MEMORY VERSE

Jesus…said to him, "Zacchaeus, come down."
~ Luke 19:5

WHAT YOU NEED

- page 78, duplicated
- crayons
- glue
- tree leaves or green paper

Jesus…said to him,
"Zacchaeus, come down."
Luke 19:5

BEFORE CLASS

Duplicate a pattern page for each child. Gather some leaves, or cut up pieces of green paper. Make a sample craft to show the children.

WHAT TO DO

1. Introduce the lesson by telling the story from Luke 19:1-10. Say, **Zacchaeus was happy to know Jesus. We are happy to know Jesus, too.**
2. Show the children the sample craft.
3. Distribute a pattern page to each child.
4. Say the memory verse.
5. Have the children color the page.
6. Show how to glue leaves or green paper onto the tree.
7. Discuss ways we can know Jesus better (Sunday school, prayer, reading the Bible, etc.)

EXTRA TIME

Provide real bark to glue onto the tree along with the leaves. (Glue the page to construction paper for sturdiness.)

Put some leaves in the tree where Zacchaeus is sitting. Zacchaeus climbed the tree so he could see Jesus.

Jesus...said to him,
"Zacchaeus, come down."
Luke 19:5

The People Praise Jesus

Mark 11:1-11

WHAT YOU NEED

- page 80, duplicated
- crayons
- tape
- hole punch
- yarn

BEFORE CLASS

Duplicate a pattern page for each child. Cut three 1" x 8" strips of paper for each child. Cut a 20" length of yarn for each child. Make a sample craft to show the children.

WHAT TO DO

1. Introduce the lesson by telling the story from Mark 11:1-11. Say, **The people were happy to see Jesus. They loudly praised Jesus. We can praise Jesus, too.**
2. Show the children the sample craft.
3. Distribute a pattern page to each child.
4. Say the memory verse.
5. Have the children tape the three paper strips to the back of the page at the bottom.
6. Have the students color the page.
7. Help the children fold the page into a triangle shape and tape the edge.
8. Punch two holes along the top edge and thread yarn through for a hanger. Say, **When you hang up your windsock at home, remember to praise Jesus.**

EXTRA TIME

Instead of paper strips, have the children tape yarn, ribbon or crepe paper to the bottom edge of the windsock. Then have the children glue glitter inside the words THEY and HOSANNA, and inside the palm leaf.

Jesus rode a donkey in Jerusalem.
People waved palms and
shouted, "Hosanna!"

Those who followed shouted, "Hosanna!" Mark 11:9

HOSANNA

SHOUTED

THEY

The Widow Gives All
Mark 12:41-44

MEMORY VERSE

She...put in everything.
~ Mark 12:44

She...put in everything.
Mark 12:44

WHAT YOU NEED

- page 82, duplicated
- crayons
- glue
- aluminum foil
- cloth or tissue pieces

BEFORE CLASS

Duplicate pattern page for each child. Make a sample craft to show the children.

WHAT TO DO

1. Introduce the lesson by telling the story from Mark 12:41-44. Say, **The woman gave all she had because she loved God. We can show God our love by giving our money to the church.**
2. Show the children the sample craft.
3. Distribute a pattern page to each child.
4. Say the memory verse.
5. Have the children tear a bit of foil and glue it to the front of the offering box.
6. Show how to glue a bit of cloth or tissue to the woman's robe.
7. Have the children color the picture. Discuss other ways we can show our love for God.

EXTRA TIME

Make a framed picture by gluing the page to a larger sheet of construction paper. Punch two holes at the top of the page and thread a length of yarn through for a hanger.

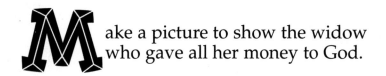 **M**ake a picture to show the widow who gave all her money to God.

She...put in everything.
Mark 12:44

Jesus Is Crucified
Matthew 27:32-61

MEMORY VERSE

They led him away to crucify him.
~ Matthew 27:31

WHAT YOU NEED

- page 84, duplicated
- 9" paper plates
- crayons
- safety scissors
- glue
- hole punch
- yarn

BEFORE CLASS

Duplicate a pattern page for each child. For younger children, cut the circle from the page. Make a sample craft to show the children.

WHAT TO DO

1. Introduce the lesson by telling about the arrest, trial and crucifixion of Jesus from Matthew 27:32-61. Say, **Everything Jesus did was to show us how much God loves us.**
2. Show the children the sample craft.
3. Distribute a pattern page to each child.
4. Say the memory verse.
5. Have the children cut out the circle from the page.
6. They should color all shapes with a dot brown.
7. Help the children glue the circle in the center of the plate.
8. Go around and punch a hole in the top of the plaque and thread a length of yarn through it. Tie for a hanger. Say, **When you see your cross, remember that God sent Jesus because He loves us.**

EXTRA TIME

Have the children color the spaces without a dot yellow. After gluing the circle to the plate, allow the children to decorate the edge of the plate with crayons or markers.

Make a cross plaque to help you remember that Jesus died on a cross for our sins.

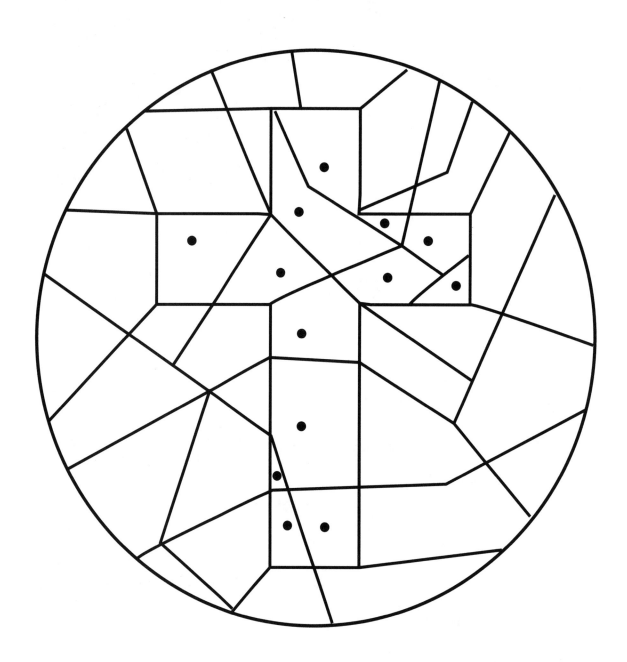

He Is Risen!
Mark 16:1-14

WHAT YOU NEED

- page 86, duplicated
- heavy white paper or card stock
- crayons
- safety scissors
- tape

BEFORE CLASS

Duplicate a pattern page onto heavy white paper or card stock for each child. For younger children, cut the strips from the page. Make a sample craft to show the children.

WHAT TO DO

1. Introduce the lesson by telling the story from Mark 16:1-14. Say, **We praise God because Jesus rose from the dead. Thank You, God!**
2. Show the children the sample craft.
3. Distribute a pattern page to each child.
4. Say the memory verse.
5. Have the children cut apart the page on the bold lines.
6. Allow the students to trace the word RISEN and color the baton.
7. Show how to fold the baton on the dashed lines and tape the edges.
8. Have the children wave their batons and shout, "Thank You, God! Jesus has risen!"

EXTRA TIME

Before assembling the batons, have the children cut and tape several lengths of yarn or shiny ribbon hanging from the inside edges.

ake a praise baton to celebrate that Jesus has risen.

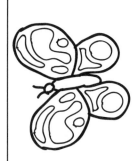

tape

He has RISEN!

He has RISEN!

tape

The Church Begins
Acts Chapter 2

MEMORY VERSE

They devoted themselves to...fellowship.
~ Acts 2:42

WHAT YOU NEED

- page 88, duplicated
- safety scissors
- crayons
- tape

BEFORE CLASS

Duplicate a pattern page for each child. For younger children, cut out the church shape. Make a sample craft to show the children.

WHAT TO DO

1. Introduce the lesson by telling the story of the first church from Acts chapter 2. Say, **The first church met together just like we meet at church each week. We can worship and share together just like the first church did.**
2. Show the children the sample craft.
3. Distribute a pattern page to each child.
4. Say the memory verse.
5. Have the children cut out the church shape.
6. Allow the children to color the church.
7. Help the children fold and tape the church as shown.
8. Discuss ways the church can worship and share, such as praying and learning together, praising in song and sharing food and money.

EXTRA TIME

Have the children cut out the windows. Then have them glue the flattened pattern to brightly-colored construction paper. After the glue dries, they should cut out the church, color it and then fold and tape it. The colored paper will show through the windows to look like stained glass.

ake a church to remember that Christians in the early church were devoted to coming together. We love to come together as a church today.

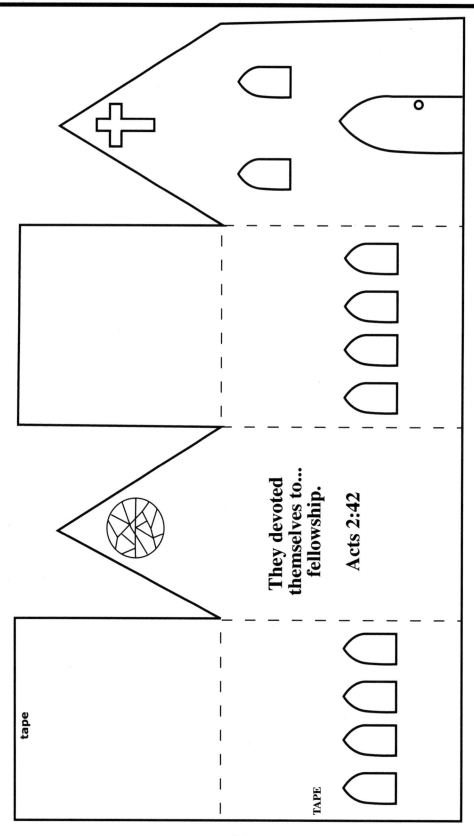

They devoted themselves to... fellowship.

Acts 2:42

tape

TAPE

Jesus Changes Saul
Acts 9:1-19

MEMORY VERSE

He got up and was baptized.
~ Acts 9:18

He got up and was baptized.
Acts 9:18

WHAT YOU NEED

- page 90, duplicated
- crayons
- glue
- aluminum foil or yellow construction paper

BEFORE CLASS

Duplicate a pattern page for each child. Make a sample craft to show the children.

WHAT TO DO

1. Introduce the lesson by telling the story from Acts 9:1-19. Say, **When Saul learned about Jesus, he went to tell others. We can tell others about Jesus, too.**
2. Show the children the sample craft.
3. Distribute a pattern page to each child.
4. Say the memory verse.
5. Have the children color all of the picture except the light beam.
6. Show how to tear pieces of foil or yellow paper and glue it on the light beam shape.
7. Have the children help retell the story while they hold their pictures.

EXTRA TIME

Have the children trim about an inch around the edge of the picture with safety scissors. Then glue the picture to a sheet of construction paper for a frame.

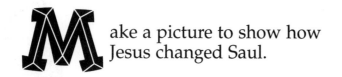 ake a picture to show how Jesus changed Saul.

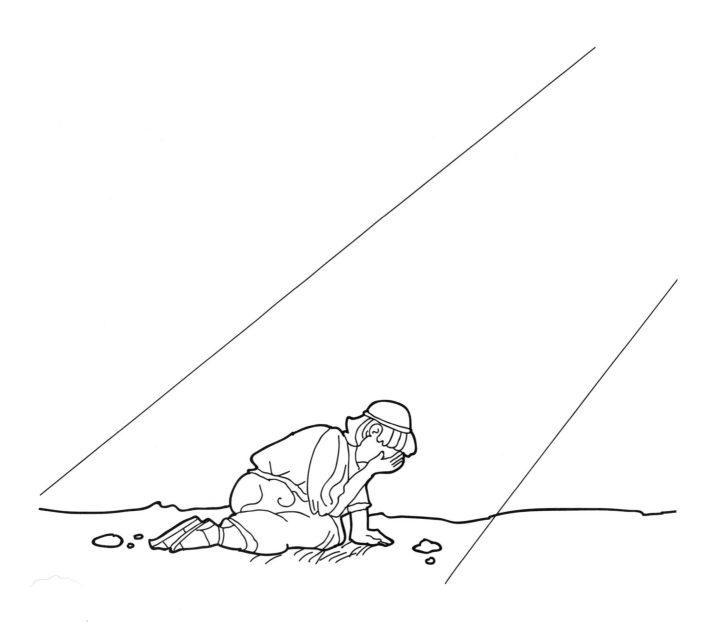

He got up and was baptized.
Acts 9:18

Paul & Silas Praise God
Acts 16:16-40

> ### MEMORY VERSE
>
> *Paul and Silas were praying and singing...to God.*
> ~ Acts 16:25

WHAT YOU NEED

- page 92, duplicated
- crayons
- safety scissors
- tape

BEFORE CLASS

Duplicate a pattern page for each child. For younger children, cut the six strips from the page. Make a sample craft to show the children.

WHAT TO DO

1. Introduce the lesson by telling the story from Acts 16:16-40. Say, **Even though Paul and Silas were in prison, they still praised God. We also can praise God even when we have troubles.**
2. Show the children the sample craft.
3. Distribute a pattern page to each child.
4. Say the memory verse.
5. Have the children cut out the six strips.
6. After the children color the strips, show how to form a chain with them.
7. Have the children hold their "chains." Say, **When we have troubles, we can still praise God.** Sing a favorite praise song with the children. Have them shake their chains as they sing.

EXTRA TIME

Provide plain paper and scissors. Have the children cut more strips. Alternate the plain strips with the Scripture strips to form a longer chain. Retell the Bible story as the children work on their chains.

Make a praise God chain to remember that we can praise God at all times.

Acts 16:16-40

I

CAN

PRAISE

AT

ALL

TIMES

An Angel Helps Peter

Acts 12:1-17

MEMORY VERSE

An angel of the Lord appeared.
~ Acts 12:7

WHAT YOU NEED

- page 94, duplicated
- crayons

BEFORE CLASS

Duplicate a pattern page for each child. Make a sample craft to show the children.

WHAT TO DO

1. Introduce the lesson by telling the story of Peter's miraculous escape from prison, found in Acts. 12:1-17. Say, **God sent an angel to help Peter get out of prison. God always finds a way to help us.**
2. Show the children the sample craft.
3. Distribute a pattern page to each child.
4. Say the memory verse.
5. Help the children fold the scene, as shown. Say, **Peter is in prison.** Open the fold, then say, **Look, now Peter is out of prison. Who helped him? It was God's angel!**
6. Have the children color the pictures. Encourage the children to retell the Bible story using the folding picture. Prepare them to be able to tell the story at home.

EXTRA TIME

Sing the song below to the tune of "Farmer in the Dell."
God sent His angel.
God sent His angel.
The angel helped Peter leave the jail.
God sent His angel.

ake a folding picture to tell the story of God's angel helping Peter get out of prison.

An angel of the Lord appeared. Acts 12:7

John Sees Heaven
Book of Revelation

WHAT YOU NEED

- page 96, duplicated
- crayons
- safety scissors
- tape
- paper towel tubes

BEFORE CLASS

Duplicate a pattern page for each child. For younger children, cut the page apart on the solid line. Make a sample craft to show the children.

WHAT TO DO

1. Introduce the lesson by telling the story of John seeing heaven in a vision from the book of Revelation. Say, **God allowed John to see what heaven is like so John could write about it in the Bible.**
2. Show the children the sample craft.
3. Distribute a pattern page to each child.
4. Say the memory verse.
5. Have the children cut the page apart on the solid line.
6. Allow the children to color the scenes as they wish.
7. Help them wrap the scene around a paper towel tube and tape at the edges. Tape at least one piece in each end to hold the scene onto the tube.
8. Have the children look through their telescopes. Ask, **What do you see? God allowed John to see heaven in a dream so we could learn about heaven by reading the Bible.**

EXTRA TIME

Talk about each picture in the scene. Say, **Who do you think sits on this throne? Who do you think will live in a mansion?**

God allowed John to see what heaven is like. What do you see through your telescope?

He made it known by sending his angel to…John. Revelation 1:1

John Saw Heaven